Dear Heather —
Thank you for loving my daughter! Sari's my heart in this book. :)
I pray God ministers to you as you read.
Sincerely,
Rebecca

Rebecca Pearce

While You Are Steeping

God-Thoughts for the Ordinary Woman

Rebecca Pearce

WESTBOW PRESS®
A DIVISION OF THOMAS NELSON
& ZONDERVAN

Copyright © 2021 Rebecca Pearce.

All rights reserved. No part of this book may be used or reproduced by any means, graphic, electronic, or mechanical, including photocopying, recording, taping or by any information storage retrieval system without the written permission of the author, except in the case of brief quotations embodied in critical articles and reviews.

This book is a work of non-fiction. Unless otherwise noted, the author and the publisher make no explicit guarantees as to the accuracy of the information contained in this book, and in some cases, names of people and places have been altered to protect their privacy.

WestBow Press books may be ordered through booksellers or by contacting:

WestBow Press
A Division of Thomas Nelson & Zondervan
1663 Liberty Drive
Bloomington, IN 47403
www.westbowpress.com
844-714-3454

Because of the dynamic nature of the Internet, any web addresses or links contained in this book may have changed since publication and may no longer be valid. The views expressed in this work are solely those of the author and do not necessarily reflect the views of the publisher, and the publisher hereby disclaims any responsibility for them.

Any people depicted in stock imagery provided by Getty Images are models, and such images are being used for illustrative purposes only. Certain stock imagery © Getty Images.

Scripture quotations taken from The Holy Bible, New International Version® NIV®. Copyright © 1973, 1978, 1984, 2011 by Biblica, Inc. TM. Used by permission. All rights reserved worldwide.

Scripture quotations taken from The Message. Copyright © 1993, 1994, 1995, 1996, 2000, 2001, 2002. Used by permission of NavPress Publishing Group.

Scripture quotations taken from the New King James Version®. Copyright © 1982 by Thomas Nelson. Used by permission. All rights reserved.

Scripture quotations taken from the New American Standard Bible®. Copyright © 1960, 1962, 1963, 1968, 1971, 1972, 1973, 1975, 1977, 1995 by The Lockman Foundation. Used by permission. www.Lockman.org.

ISBN: 978-1-6642-1535-1 (sc)
ISBN: 978-1-6642-1534-4 (hc)
ISBN: 978-1-6642-1536-8 (e)

Library of Congress Control Number: 2020924196

Print information available on the last page.

WestBow Press rev. date: 1/14/2021

Contents

Acknowledgments ix
Introduction xi
Preface xiii

I Meet Him in My Dailiness

My Home, My Eden 1
The Light of His Presence 4
Capacity 8
Clean, But Not All 11
Living a Life of Readiness 14
Lessons from My Plants 17
Sometimes You Need a New Pot 20
Warfare 23

I Meet Him in My Struggles

Just for Today, Lord 29
Exhausted Yet Still Pursuing 32
I Know You by Name 35
He Sees Me 39
Hiding by the Baggage 44
The Life Well Lived 47

I Meet Him in My Loneliness

Flat Days 53
Soul Wounds 56
A – Stigma – Tism 59
The Loneliest Hour 63

I Meet Him in My Grief

Five Days a Grandma 69
Song for September 72
When Love Dies 76
You Don't Owe Me 79
Here Lies a Faithful Man 82
On the Passing of a New Friend 86
At Year's End 89

I Meet Him in My Restlessness

I Wait 97
Abba's Daughters 100
On Earth As It Is in Heaven 103
My Grown-Up Christmas 109
I Cannot Fail 113

Epilogue 117
References 121

What I'm trying to do here is get you to relax, not be so preoccupied with *getting* so you can respond to God's *giving*. People who don't know God and the way he works fuss over these things, but you know both God and how he works. Steep yourself in God-reality, God-initiative, God-provisions. You'll find all your everyday human concerns will be met. Don't be afraid of missing out. You're my dearest friends! The Father wants to give you the very kingdom itself.

—Luke 12:29–32 (*The Message*)

Acknowledgments

This book is dedicated to my husband, Carson, for his unwavering support throughout our forty-three years of marriage; to my father, Jim Johnson, for his never-failing confidence in me to be able to do whatever I set my mind to do; and to Bob Mather, my mentor in Christ, who challenged me to set goals and taught me how to achieve them.

Many thanks go to my girlfriends and my children—Jessica, Brian, and Angela—for being my lifelong cheerleaders and prayer partners! I want to especially recognize and thank my daughter, Jessica (Pearce) Fields, for her keen insights and wisdom in editing these pieces with me, along with my dear friend, Robin Kilchrist, for being my "second pair of eyes" as a proofreader. I wish to express my appreciation to my daughter, Angela (Pearce) Vanderwerf, for her beautiful photography work in producing my author photo. Finally, I want to thank the entire WestBow Press team for their expertise in bringing this long-awaited dream of publishing my book to reality.

Introduction

Why a mug? Why not a delicate teacup? I chose a mug because I am a mug person. I love going to the homes of friends who bring out their tea service, or their finest china, because that is a special occasion. But mugs represent to me the ordinariness of life. A mug of tea accompanies me when I check my email, when I do the finances, or when I read the news. It's part of the routine of my life.

I believe the Lord wants our time with him to quit being a special event. I believe he wants to be included in the mundane parts of our lives as well.

Why the title? My husband came up with the title as I was telling him I ought to write a book about all the things you can get done while a cup of tea is steeping (three to five minutes). I was talking about making good use of my time and how I can make the bed, or empty the dishwasher, or sort through junk mail, while I anticipate a good cup of tea.

Then I began to write short vignettes about the ordinary and the poignant things happening in my life, and I decided to put the two together. Thus it became a book of "God-thoughts" that could be pondered over a cup of tea or coffee.

Why that scripture verse? I stumbled upon the verse about being steeped in "God-reality" while looking up a Bible verse online once, and it stuck with me as the perfect passage to include in this book. This definition comes from the Merriam-Webster online dictionary:

Steep suggests either the extraction of an essence (as of tea leaves) by the liquid or the imparting of a quality (as a color) to the thing immersed <*steep* the tea for five minutes>[1]

The Father wants to impart the character of Christ to us as we immerse ourselves in his presence. We will never fully come to know him or become like him by "dunking the tea bag" a few times. Yes, the water may turn brown, and it may resemble tea, but it's a weak version of what it was meant to be. It does not have the satisfying richness imparted by time and patient waiting.

---

[1] "Steep," Merriam-Webster.com, accessed 7 November 2019, https://www.merriam-webster.com/dictionary/steep?utm_campaign=sd&utm_medium=serp&utm_source=jsonld.

Preface

In My Middle Years

In my middle years, I celebrate my laugh lines for the joys I've experienced, and I honor my creases for the sorrows I've weathered. Without these markers, my life would appear a blank slate with memories erased, victories forgotten, and history rewritten.

In my middle years, I choose to fight poverty, injustice, and ignorance instead of age spots, frown lines, and belly fat. I choose to forgo the illusion of youth so that children in other countries can live out their own childhood. If I must "fight," let it be for something lasting that will make a difference in this world long after this spirit house of mine gives way to the inevitability of decay.

In my middle years, I dare to believe that one person can make a difference in this world. I believe that my voice is unique and that it's worth my effort to call forth the best in others.

> "When he was at the table with them, he took bread, gave thanks, broke it and began to give it to them. Then their eyes were opened and they recognized him."
>
> —Luke 24:30–31

I Meet Him in My Dailiness

My Home, My Eden

Just for an hour, Lord, let me enjoy my
home with everything in its place. I want
to soak in its orderliness so that my
internal world can also feel at peace.

Let me revel in freshly made beds,
sparkling bathrooms, tidy countertops,
and glossy floors. For one hour, let me
be queen of my garden and take pleasure
in its array.

Is this how you felt when you
stepped back from all your creating and
said, "This is very good"?

Father, you created order out of chaos, and from that order sprang forth life and beauty. Lord, may the condition of my heart and the condition of my home bring life, beauty, and peace to me and others.

Time to Steep

- In what tangible areas of my life do I find peace and beauty? My home? My workspace? My garden?
- How can I partner with God in those settings to allow my heart and mind to become a restful, delightful place for my own well-being and the good of others?

For Further Steeping

Genesis 1:31; Colossians 3:15; 1 Corinthians 14:33

While You Are Steeping

The Light of His Presence

> Many, Lord, are asking, "Who will bring us prosperity?" Let the light of your face shine on us.
>
> —Psalm 4:6

I suffer from seasonal affective disorder (SAD), so this year, I finally bought a light box. In case you're not familiar with what a light box does, it simulates the intensity of the sun and increases the serotonin level in your body, which affects mood. I've already seen the difference it has made here in Alaska, where daylight and sunlight have become more and more precious commodities as the winter days grow shorter. The directions say to sit nine to fourteen inches away. They also say you do not have to look constantly at the light box; glancing up occasionally is enough. The main requirements are that your eyes are open and that your face is bathed in the light.

This morning, I decided to give the light my full attention. Instead of reading or trying to do a task, I sat and sipped tea; then I savored my three squares of dark chocolate while looking steadily into the light. I felt myself relax and become calm, and I just allowed myself to be fully aware.

When the light box turned off, I looked around at my well-lit home, including all the Christmas lights that were on, and everything seemed like distant, dim lanterns instead of the blazing cheeriness they had projected only fifteen minutes before.

Immediately, an old chorus, and then an old hymn, came to mind.

> When I look into your holiness, when I gaze into your loveliness,

When all things that surround become shadows in
the light of you ... [2]

Turn your eyes upon Jesus.
Look full in his wonderful face,
And the things of earth will grow strangely dim
In the light of his glory and grace.[3]

God does not call us to glance occasionally in his direction. He calls us to turn our eyes on him, to look intently, to gaze steadily, and to allow his radiance to bathe our being and permeate our souls. He calls us to the light of his presence to help us keep this world, with all of its allure, in its proper perspective.

Father, may I purpose in my heart to give myself, fully present, to the light of your face. Help me resist the urge to multitask when I spend time with you. Let me become so aware of your presence that even the best things in my life take second place to you.

---

[2] Cathy Perrin and Wayne Perrin, "When I Look into Your Holiness," © 1981. Integrity's Hosanna! Music. Used with permission.
[3] Helen Howarth Lemmel, "The Heavenly Vision (Turn Your Eyes upon Jesus)," 1918. Public domain.

Time to Steep

- What steps can I take to become more intentional in my quiet time with God?
- What verse can I memorize to help me meditate on God?

For Further Steeping

Psalm 4:6; 1 John 1:7; 2 Corinthians 3:18

Capacity

I'm sitting at my computer, waiting for an enormous file to finish downloading, while every other task I attempt is frozen or delayed for a minute upon each keystroke. My computer is old and slow and simply doesn't have the capacity to handle the amount of information it's receiving right now.

Oftentimes, I feel just like my old computer. As I'm facing a huge challenge, it takes all my energy, and I become sluggish, overwhelmed, or even completely exhausted. In those times, I feel I have nothing left to give, and I struggle to hear from my heavenly Father. But more and more, I'm learning to recognize that it's not about me and what I can do or give. It's all about him and the life that he imparts to me through Jesus. His Spirit gives me the capacity to do and be more than I ever could on my own. I rely on him for my strength and trust him for daily renewal.

God has said in his Word that he will speak to me through his Spirit. Yet *his thoughts are not my thoughts, and my ways are not his ways* (Isaiah 55:8). He has also told me that *new wine cannot be contained in old wineskins* (Matthew 9:17). In other words, I need to be *renewed in the attitude of my mind* so that I have the ability to receive his thoughts, comprehend them, and act on what he's said (Ephesians 4:23). Thankfully, in both my spirit and my mind, he's able to increase my capacity.

Father, I'm feeling lethargic today. I know that you're speaking, but my mind feels frozen and my responses are lagging. My processor is so slow, Lord. I need an upgrade! I need an expansion of my mind to grasp your thoughts. Transform my mind so that I can understand your ways.

Time to Steep

- In what ways can I draw closer to the Lord so that he can renew my mind, expand my ability to hear his voice, and restore my spirit?
- Is there any area of my beliefs or reasoning where I'm preventing God's Spirit from having full access?

For Further Steeping

John 15:5; 1 John 5:12; Colossians 1:29; 2 Peter 1:3; Philippians 4:11–13; John 14:26; John 16:13; Isaiah 55:8–9; Matthew 9:17; Ephesians 4:22–24; Romans 12:2; Luke 24:45; Ephesians 3:20–21

Clean, But Not All

As part of preparation to sell our home, I had self-cleaned the oven, bought new burner pans for the stove, and cleaned under the stove top, and then I was cleaning the "dab" of grease off the top of the range hood.

As a matter of habit, I've kept the range hood wiped down from dust pretty often. I thought it was clean and just needed a touch-up.

For whatever reason, I stuck my head *under* the range hood to wipe off what looked like a little dust, and to my horror, it was *covered* with grease. It was disgusting. The light bulb was yellow and furry! How had I not seen that before?

The light bulb and light bulb cover came out, the grease screen came out, and I started spraying everything in sight with grease remover!

As I cleaned and alternately berated myself, the Holy Spirit was speaking a scripture to my heart.

"Search me, O God … and see if *there is any* wicked way in me" (Psalm 139:23–24 NKJV).

Father, I invite you to shine a spotlight on my life. I'm not content to just look good to others if there are things in my life that need a good scrubbing. Wash me, cleanse me—be thorough, but be gentle—and leave me intact and shining.

Time to Steep

- Although I daily "bathe" with the water of the Word, are there things I'm just wiping over, smug in my self-righteousness but not really seeing how the world and its ways are clinging to me?
- Are there habits and attitudes in me that obscure the light of Christ?

For Further Steeping

Psalm 139:23–24 NKJV; John 13:10; Matthew 23:25–28; Ephesians 5:26

Living a Life of Readiness

I was just reading in Ephesians 6 today about the armor of God. It seems like I have a pretty good understanding of most of the pieces of the armor, but verse 15 was unclear to me: "And with your feet fitted with the readiness that comes from the gospel of peace."

Readiness. I had an illustration of that today before we left for the Father's Day picnic. A man drove by to see our house, which was for sale; found my husband, Carson, outside working on the lawn; and asked to come in to see it. Normally, we were not supposed to allow that, but it was our real estate agent's day off because of the holiday; and since the man had already spoken with the agent, we felt it would be all right.

Carson called sweetly into the house, "There's someone here to see the house."

I called politely back, "Give me five minutes!" Then I scurried around, flicking lights on, stuffing glasses into the dishwasher, and opening blinds. (Our agent had said to make our home as light as possible and to especially turn the lights on in dark rooms.)

Readiness. I was able to meet the man's request because I'd been working hard all week to have the house virtually spotless. We had straightened the house before church also, so it was literally in a "five-minutes-to-perfect" stage.

I wonder how ready I am when the enemy is plotting an attack against me. I wonder how ready I am when God brings me opportunities to minister. Am I living life "with my shoes on"?

Father, I want to be found ready. May I be continually filled with your Holy Spirit and your Word so I'm prepared at a moment's notice for anything that comes my way, whether it's the enemy's attack, an opportunity to minister, or a chance to give you thanks.

Time to Steep

- Am I maintaining my internal house so that I can face anything that comes my way?
- What steps can I take today to begin to clear the clutter in my life, my mind, my heart?

For Further Steeping

Ephesians 6:10–18; Matthew 25:1–13; 2 Timothy 4:2

Lessons from My Plants

On a road trip, I was reading a copy of *Discipleship Journal* magazine. The entire issue was focused on "The Fruitful Life." I read this poignant passage: "Fruitbearing is a process. A new plant does not immediately bear fruit. First, the plant needs enough nutrients for *life*. Then, if it has enough nutrients to stay alive, it needs more for *growth*. Finally, if it has enough nutrients to stay alive and grow, it then needs more for *bearing fruit and reproducing*."[4]

I immediately thought of my two hanging baskets on the porch. Both had been pruned back, but only one was producing "fruit" (flowers). One was flourishing; one was floundering. I realized that the sickly one was receiving the same amount of water as the healthy one; it was also receiving the same amount of fertilizer. But somehow, the sickly one was not retaining the nutrients I was providing it. In essence, the water poured right through the pot. At best, the roots caught a sip on the way out.

I recognized that the plant was only receiving enough nutrients to stay alive, but it was not capable of either growth or producing fruit.

When I returned home, I immediately got the scissors and ruthlessly pruned the plant back even more. Then I decided to try something: I only gave the plant enough water so that it didn't rush out the bottom. I waited, and then I gave it a bit more. The plant began looking healthier, and fresh blooms appeared on the uppermost growth.

I've realized some things about my life too. There have been times in my Christian walk when I've barely taken in enough of the Word to keep a spiritual pulse. Those were seasons of barrenness—often of my own making. At other times, I was drinking in much of the Word

---

[4] Chuck Broughton, "Fruit Without Frustration: Adventures in the Great Commission," *Discipleship Journal,* May–June 2005. Used with permission.

but—like the proverbial sip out of the fire hose—I was retaining little of what I took in. Then there have been seasons when I've drawn in the Word a little at a time and I've soaked in it, extracting the life that I needed. Those seemed to be my periods of greatest growth.

Father, may I examine my life to see if I'm abiding in Christ and your Word enough to bear fruit and reproduce your life in others.

Time to Steep

- What season am I currently in: a season of "life support," growth, or reproduction?
- What changes can I make in my approach to Bible study that will help me internalize it more so that I'm bearing fruit?

For Further Steeping

John 15:1–8; 2 Corinthians 13:5; 2 Peter 1:5–10

Sometimes You Need a New Pot

When I moved into my new home in Texas, I inherited two pots of petunias that the previous owners had left. In the center of the largest pot sat a single marigold plant. It has produced a few blooms since I've lived here but, by and large, the stalk has sat empty, surrounded by a sea of scarlet petunias. It has grown taller but without blooms.

Though I'm a novice when it comes to tending plants, I've learned a few things. A plant becomes rootbound when there is no more room in the pot to contain the roots. The only way for the plant to continue to grow in health is to transplant it to a bigger pot. Yesterday, I removed the marigold plant and gave it its own pot, and that reminded me of some things that are true about our lives.

Sometimes you need a new pot.

There are times when we've been in a specific job, ministry, church, or other situation where we feel we've either stopped growing, stopped producing fruit, or have no more room for our roots to spread. We often experience emotions like discouragement, apathy, and discontent, or we even tend to become critical.

What this may mean is that God is calling us to a position of greater responsibility within our workplace, church, or community; or it may mean he's moving us to another place entirely where there is room to grow. Although the old saying "Bloom where you are planted" has truth to it, the greater truth is that—except for the hardiest plants—conditions need to be right in order to bloom.

Before we had even considered moving from our home in Alaska, my grown son made a very profound comment to my husband. He pondered, "I wonder what God could do through Mom if she wasn't always having to fight her environment." Having lived in Alaska for twenty-six years—suffering from both Seasonal Affective Disorder (SAD) and clinical depression, and never fully adjusting to the cold and the dark—much of my emotional and spiritual energy was spent just trying to cope.

Sometimes you need a new pot.

If your joy begins to dissipate or disappear entirely from pursuits that have previously brought you fulfillment, challenge, and success, perhaps it's time to ask the Lord if he's transplanting you so that you can be of greater usefulness and wider influence for the kingdom of God.

Father, I want to experience your abundant life in the here and now. If you are moving me on to something new, please help me to recognize it. Help me to patiently wait for you to *"hasten it in its time"* (Isaiah 60:22 NKJV). Let me grow and bear good fruit in keeping with new joy in my heart.

Time to Steep

- Am I experiencing discontent, discouragement, or apathy in any area of my life?
- Is there an area where the Lord may be ready to move me into a "bigger pot"?

For Further Steeping

Psalm 92:12–15; Isaiah 55:12–13; Isaiah 60:22 NKJV; Matthew 13:1–9

Warfare

It's *warfare* in Texas! Daily, unrelenting warfare.

Our enemies are everywhere! They're tiny; they're large; they're harmless; they're poisonous. Ants in the windowsill, a spider in the kitchen, a cricket in the closet, wasps in the trees, fire ants in the grass, killer bees on the flowers. When did life become so hostile here? Morning and evening, "my hero" husband sets out with his chemical weapons. He hunts them; he finds their hiding places; he destroys their access to our home.

Would that we were so diligent rooting out the access of the enemy of our souls.

How easy it is to tolerate a wrong attitude, a destructive habit, or a secret sin, not realizing that it is slowly taking over. Yet God calls us to get rid of things like *"anger, rage, malice, slander, and filthy language"* (Colossians 3:8); to *"demolish strongholds"* in our thinking (2 Corinthians 10:4); and to *"put to death the misdeeds of the body"* (Romans 8:13)—to take action against whatever threatens to undermine our relationship with him. Those are *fighting* words! It's *warfare time!*

Father, help me to draw near to you, *"resist the devil,"* and watch him flee (James 4:7–8a)! Let me no longer tolerate *"the sin that so easily entangles [me]"* but focus intently on you, *"Jesus, the pioneer and perfecter of [my] faith"* (Hebrews 12:1–2a). Let me deal a death blow to the sin in my life through the power of your Spirit and enjoy living victoriously free in you!

Time to Steep

- Is there any area in my life where I've been giving the enemy access to my soul or mind?
- In what ways can I turn to the Lord instead of to that sin or habit?

For Further Steeping

Colossians 3:8; 2 Corinthians 10:4; Romans 8:13; Ephesians 6:12–13; James 4:7–8a; Hebrews 12:1–2a

> "'Take courage! It is I. Don't be afraid.' Then he climbed into the boat with them, and the wind died down."
>
> —Mark 6:50b–51

I Meet Him in My Struggles

Just for Today, Lord

Just for today, Lord,
May I really believe
That each day has enough
Troubles of its own.

May I not borrow possibilities
From tomorrow or next week or next month,
And may I not resurrect yesterday's failures
Or heartaches to compound the challenges
Of today.

Just for today, Lord,
May I really believe
That your grace is enough—
That manna comes each day,
And your supply will never run short.

Just for today, Lord,
May I look to you
For the strength and wisdom I need
To meet the tasks and tests today brings.

And when the day is done,
May I lay my head on the pillow
And bask in the peace
Of your watchful embrace.[5]

---

[5] This poem is dedicated to my father, Jim Johnson, who taught me how to trust my heavenly Father.

Father, this poem is my honest prayer to you. (Read the poem out loud to God.)

Time to Steep

- In what circumstances am I struggling to trust God?
- Which scriptures can I meditate on to keep my heart and mind at peace?

For Further Steeping

Matthew 6:34; John 14:1–2; 2 Corinthians 12:9; Exodus 16 (esp. vs. 18 and 31); Matthew 6:7–13; Isaiah 26:3; Psalm 119:165; John 16:33; Proverbs 3:5; Isaiah 30:15; Psalm 4:8; Philippians 4:6–7

Exhausted Yet Still Pursuing

Just now, I've had one of those wonderful moments of insight that the Lord gives—when he opens your eyes to see something new in the passage that you've "read a thousand times."

I was reading the story of Gideon's defeat of the Midianites in Judges, chapters 7 and 8. The first insight that struck me came while pondering the familiar verse 7:6: "Three hundred of them drank from cupped hands, lapping like dogs. All the rest got down on their knees to drink." I stopped to picture it again, and I looked down at my NIV note, which said this: "The 300 remained on their feet, prepared for any emergency."[6]

It was about *vigilance*. God was looking for vigilant warriors. They didn't wait until they were engaged in battle; they stayed alert, looking for signs of the enemy.

The second insight came in 8:4: "Gideon and his three hundred men, **exhausted yet keeping up the pursuit,** came to the Jordan and crossed it" (emphasis mine).

Oh, how I understand that phrase! I feel like I have *lived* in this verse for so many years I could write a book about it—*exhausted yet keeping up the pursuit.*

Dear ones, I know that many of you are in this situation right now. Be encouraged by the Lord. He looks at you with great favor. You were handpicked and sought out by the Lord to engage the enemy in battle because he knows you are **fearless, vigilant, and persevering.**

Don't become discouraged in the battle. You *will* win because the Lord has given you the victory, and because *he believes in you* and the quality of person that you are.

---

[6] Taken from *The NIV Study Bible New International Version.* Copyright © 1985 by Zondervan. Used by permission of Zondervan. www.zondervan.com.

Father, I am so weary from the battle. I don't feel like I can go on anymore, but I know you can. I know you are *"Christ in [me], the hope of glory"* (Colossians 1:27). I believe you see my vigilance, and you know that I'm ready for whatever is next. Since I've *"done everything, to stand"* (Ephesians 6:13), help me stand firm, knowing *"the battle is [yours]"* (1 Samuel 17:47).

Time to Steep

- What battle do I find myself in right now?
- What are some promises from the Bible I can claim in my situation?

For Further Steeping

Judges 7:6, 8:4; Colossians 1:27; Ephesians 6:13; 2 Chronicles 20:15; 1 Samuel 17:47

I Know You by Name

> Do not fear, for I have redeemed you; I have called you by name; you are Mine! When you pass through the waters, I will be with you; And through the rivers, they will not overflow you. When you walk through the fire, you will not be scorched, nor will the flame burn you. For I am the Lord your God, the Holy One of Israel, your Savior.
>
> —Isaiah 43:1b–3a (NASB)

He knows my name!

In my eighth grade social studies class, there was a very good-looking boy who sat behind me. I was totally intimidated by him, and I was amazed when he actually spoke to me by name! I felt so special being noticed by one of the popular kids.

More importantly, *he* knows my name! I'm not just some cog in the cosmic wheel of God's sovereign plan. He knows who I am.

I belong to him!

I remember, as a young teen, being asked to "go steady" by my boyfriend and being given my first ID bracelet with his name on it. I *belonged* to someone; his name was engraved on a bracelet that told everyone whose I was.

In the same way, God himself has *"engraved [me] on the palms of [his] hands"* (Isaiah 49:16). I belong to him.

When I pass through the waters ... when I walk through the fire ...

There will be hardships and adversities in this life—not *if,* but *when.* However, he will be with me, just like a good husband who walks through the trials of life with the woman he loves. I *will* pass through the waters, rivers, flames, and fires of life—that part is not optional. But I *will* go through them with *him*. He is both my water-walking companion and my fourth man in the fire (Matthew 14:28–29; Daniel 3:25)! What's more, he has promised there will be an end to the trials.

I will not be overcome!

Because he has called me by name and claims me as his own, my victory is assured! I will not "get burned" by people or situations—God has said there will be no harmful, lasting effects in my life because he loves me and *works all things for my good* (Romans 8:28).

For I am the Lord your God ...

The promise of victory is based on who God is, not on who I am. I can *boast in my own weakness,* knowing where my strength and my help come from (2 Corinthians 12:9). He is my Redeemer and Savior, and at the core of it all, he is a Father who loves me, knows me by name, and calls me his own.

Father, thank you that you know me by name, by heart. You will *"never leave [me] nor forsake [me],"* even when I'm in the fight of my life (Deuteronomy 31:6). You go with me and before me, and you will lead me into the victory you've promised.

Time to Steep

- How does the knowledge of belonging to God encourage me when I'm walking through a difficult situation?
- What is one way God has demonstrated his love to me personally that I can focus on this week?

For Further Steeping

Isaiah 43:1b–3a NASB; Isaiah 41:10; Isaiah 49:16; Jeremiah 1:19; Matthew 14:22–23 and 28–29; Daniel 3:25; Deuteronomy 31:6; Romans 8:28; 2 Corinthians 12:9; Psalm 121; Psalm 118:1–16

He Sees Me

In my Bible reading plan, I was due to start Ezekiel yesterday, yet I've been feeling the increasing need to read the book of Revelation first, so I switched the order.

Having been a Christian for over forty-seven years, I've read Revelation more than a few times; and in the past, I've mumbled my way through parts of it like I sometimes do the genealogies in other books. In other words, I was doing my Christian duty but with no understanding from the Spirit.

Today I was surprised by what the Lord spoke to my heart as I read Revelation. I hope this will encourage you as it did me.

In certain Christian circles during the 1980s, it was common to berate people for using phrases like "under the circumstances" or "hanging in there." Supposedly, Christians should never be *under* their circumstances. We are victorious; we are overcomers. While this is true, I don't believe scripture ignores or negates the struggles we face or the difficulty it often takes to *be* an overcomer.

As I've freshly read Jesus's words to the seven churches, I've seen the compassion of Christ toward our individual circumstances.

To the church in Ephesus:

"I know your deeds, your hard work and your perseverance … You have persevered and have endured hardship for my name, and have not grown weary" (Revelation 2:2a–3).

To the church in Smyrna:

"I know your afflictions and your poverty—yet you are rich!" (Revelation 2:9a).

To the church in Pergamum:

"I know where you live—where Satan has his throne. Yet you remain true to my name. You did not renounce your faith in me" (Revelation 2:13a, b).

To the church in Thyatira:

"I know your deeds, your love and faith, your service and perseverance, and that you are now doing more than you did at first ... **hold on to what you have** until I come" (Revelation 2:19 and 25, emphasis mine).

To the church in Sardis:

"Yet you have a few people in Sardis who have not soiled their clothes" (Revelation 3:4a).

To the church in Philadelphia:

"I know that you have little strength, yet you have kept my word and have not denied my name ... I am coming soon. **Hold on to what you have,** so that no one will take your crown" (Revelation 3:8b and 11, emphasis mine).

To the church in Laodicea:

"I counsel you to buy from me gold refined in the fire, so you can become rich; and white clothes to wear, so you can cover your shameful nakedness; and salve to put on your eyes, so you can see. Those whom I love I rebuke and discipline" (Revelation 3:18–19a).

If I were writing a personal letter to you, this is what I would want you to know:

My dear friend,

Jesus sees the circumstances of your life. He sees the hardships you have had to endure for his sake. He sees the struggles to hold onto your integrity in the midst of a hedonistic society. He sees the struggles to maintain a walk of truth in the midst of error. He sees the struggles to maintain a passionate love for him in the midst of an apathetic church.

He sees you when you feel you are hanging on by a thread against the onslaught of life's circumstances and the continual buffeting from the enemy. My friend, *hold on*. He doesn't reserve his rewards only for those who march triumphantly through the battles of life. His rewards are also for those of us who cling to him with our last ounce of strength.

Jesus also sees you when your heart has grown cold toward him and you don't even realize it. His mercy is reaching out to you; take hold of it and he will restore you.

Your sister in Christ,
Rebecca

Father, thank you for your mercy in seeing me and accepting me as I am, right where I'm at. Thank you that you will not *snuff out a smoldering wick* (Matthew 12:20). You will preserve me and give me strength, even if it's just enough to hold onto you, my ultimate sufficiency. Lord, help me stand firm in you and be counted as one who overcomes "*by the blood of the Lamb and by the word of [my] testimony*" (Revelation 12:11).

Time to Steep

- In what area am I struggling to overcome right now?
- How have Jesus's words to the seven churches spoken encouragement to me in this area?

For Further Steeping

Revelation 2 and 3 (esp. 2:10); Hebrews 11:35b–40; Isaiah 42:3; Ephesians 6:13; Matthew 12:20; Revelation 12:11

Hiding by the Baggage

There is an amazing story in 1 Samuel, chapters 9 and 10, telling how God appointed Saul to be the first king of Israel. Of course, he only did this to acquiesce to Israel's demands, but he gave them a king nevertheless.

Not only did Saul lack the *confidence* to be the king (9:21), but he didn't *want* to be king either! It was only after the Spirit of God came upon Saul that he had the capability to fulfill his destiny (10:6 and 9).

When it came time to actually anoint Saul as king, Samuel had to go looking for him. The people of Israel asked God where Saul was. "They inquired further of the LORD, 'Has the man come here yet?'" (1 Samuel 10:22a NASB).

I love what God revealed about Saul in his reply: "So the LORD said, 'Behold, he is hiding himself by the baggage'" (1 Samuel 10:22b NASB).

It's impossible to go through life without accumulating some baggage: an abusive childhood, a failed marriage, children who disappoint us, financial failure, dashed hopes, loss of dreams, and more. It's easy to layer ourselves with these wounds and decide that, because of them, we are useful neither to God nor to anyone else. Yet God doesn't view these painful circumstances as disqualifications for doing his will. He will gladly use us as we make ourselves available to him by faith.

Father, forgive me for hiding myself by the baggage in my life. Help me step out from among this stuff and step into my calling. Thank you that *"I can do all things through Christ who strengthens me"* by the power of your Spirit within me (Philippians 4:13 NKJV).

Time to Steep

- Am I holding onto something from my past that's keeping me from moving forward in faith?
- What step can I take to trust God and release this, by his power that's within me?

For Further Steeping

1 Samuel 9 and 10; 1 Samuel 10:22 NASB; Philippians 3:13–14; Philippians 4:13 NKJV; 2 Peter 1:3

The Life Well Lived

This morning as I was reading my daily Bible readings, I realized one of the passages was the genealogy in Luke 3:21–38. Ugh! A genealogy ... okay, God, surely there is something there.

Halfway through reading obscure names that do not trip lightly off the tongue, I came across this little mention in verse 31: "the son of Nathan, the son of David ..."

Nathan? Who's Nathan? I know Solomon and Absalom and Amnon—those were some of David's "bad boys." But who is this Nathan?

Now, I haven't done an extensive Bible survey, but a quick reading of 2 Samuel 5:14 and 1 Chronicles 3:5 told me that Nathan was Solomon's brother, one of the four sons of Bathsheba.

I think Nathan was a "good boy," with no particular claim to fame that would have propelled him into the halls of scripture like some of his brothers and half-brothers. Yet here he is, listed in the genealogy of Joseph, Jesus's earthly father.

I was reminded of a discussion at a small-group meeting where one of the women was lamenting her lack of an exciting testimony. We talked about how a life well lived is a testimony of its own. It's a testimony to the power of God that is able to keep us from stumbling.

"To him who is able to keep you from stumbling and to present you before his glorious presence without fault and with great joy" (Jude 24).

God is able to use bad boys and good boys, bad girls and good girls to accomplish his purposes. We all stand in need of a Savior, whether our life has stayed on the straight and narrow or has taken large detours into places we wish we'd never been.

We neither have to be *ashamed* of where we've been nor *apologize* for never "going there."

Father, I confess that I've sometimes felt a twinge of jealousy when I've heard others share their powerful testimonies of deliverance, freedom from sin, and dramatic conversions. I'm recognizing now, though, that walking uprightly in the middle of this sinful world is a powerful witness to all. Help me not to focus on the seeming smallness of my testimony but on the greatness of my God!

Time to Steep

- Where in my life have I seen God's faithfulness to keep me from stumbling? How can I weave those experiences into my testimony?
- Whom can I look to and learn from as a role model for consistent, godly living?

For Further Steeping

Luke 3:21–38; 2 Samuel 5:14; 1 Chronicles 3:5; Jude 1:24; Psalm 23:3; Proverbs 3:21–23; Proverbs 4:11–13; 2 Timothy 1:5–6; 1 Corinthians 11:1; Hebrews 13:7

> "At my first defense, no one came to my support, but everyone deserted me. May it not be held against them. But the Lord stood at my side and gave me strength …"
>
> —2 Timothy 4:16–17a

I Meet Him in My Loneliness

Flat Days

Flat days—
Two-dimension,
Cardboard days of
Faded colors,
Muted sounds, and
Dulled emotions.

God seems distant,
Even gone.
Spirit stirrings
Dwindle to a
Faint pulse,
Void of hope or
Expectation.

Bring me back to
Third dimension—
Even fourth—
Eternal eyes to
See your work in
All my moments
As I live,
Fully present.

Father, I'm struggling today to feel—to feel joy or anger, hope or despair, love or hatred. My soul is numb, anesthetized. Yet I trust in your unseen presence like I trust in the air that I breathe. Holy Spirit of God, infuse me with your life, and make me whole again.

Time to Steep

- When has God seemed most distant to me?
- In what subtle ways did I experience his presence during that time?

For Further Steeping

Psalm 13:1–5; Psalm 22:1–3 (also Matthew 27:46); Psalm 27:7–9 and 13–14; Job 33:4

Soul Wounds

No eyes can see my wounded heart.
No ears can hear my cry.
The silence of a thousand graves
Hangs deeply in my sigh.

Would I could bare this bloody breach
That others fully know,
But caution bids me shroud myself,
My vacant eyes to show.

The scars form tight within my soul.
My movements they constrain;
Yet others see unyieldedness
And never glimpse my pain.

I tend my soul wounds valiantly
And enter Father's rest,
Yet longing for a human touch
Sits weighty on my breast.

If I could turn this flesh about,
The damage they would see;
They'd bind my wounds and hold me close,
Then lift and carry me.

Thank you, Holy Spirit, for carrying my *"wordless sighs"* to the Father (Romans 8:26 MSG). Lord, thank you that you see me and know me inside and out; nothing is hidden from you—not my smallest disappointments nor my deepest aches. You care intently, and you will comfort me. Although many don't or won't understand me, please provide me a few real friends with whom I can share the most vulnerable parts of myself. Give me the courage to be honest, and help me to heal.

Time to Steep

- When my soul has been wounded, how have I protected myself from further hurt? Did this allow me to fully heal or just distance myself from others?
- Who is someone I trust that I can share my soul wounds with?

For Further Steeping

Psalm 139:1–18; Proverbs 18:24; Isaiah 42:3; Isaiah 61:1–3; Romans 8:26–27 MSG

A – Stigma – Tism

> The human spirit can endure in sickness, but a crushed spirit who can bear?
>
> —Proverbs 18:14

astigmatism: *n*. defect of the eye producing imperfect focus[7]

stigma: *n*. 1. a brand or mark of infamy; a disgrace [8]

Imagine going to the doctor to have some debilitating symptoms checked, finding out you're very ill but can be treated, and then being told you should not tell anyone you're ill. This is what it feels like to be a Christian diagnosed with depression.

I'm not talking about feeling blue, having an off day, or being temporarily sad about something. I'm talking about clinical depression, which involves a physical change in the brain that needs to be healed through a combination of medicine, counseling, and spiritual and emotional support.

Within the church, there's a stigma attached to depression and other mental illness that's usually reserved for the likes of sexually transmitted diseases. It's something we don't like to talk about. Among the unlearned, depression is equated to spiritual or emotional weakness and a failure to "do" Christianity properly. Among the learned, there is often still the perception that a person would not have become depressed had he or she maintained faith and stayed well connected with the Lord.

I believe that the root of these attitudes is fear—fear that it could

---

[7] *The New American Webster Handy College Dictionary Third Edition* (New York: The Penguin Group, 1995), 51.
[8] *The New American Webster Handy College Dictionary Third Edition*, 647.

happen to me, fear that compels me to explain away something I don't fully understand. If I can surround myself with a list of proper behaviors and duties, then maybe I can ward off this thing called depression.

Except when I can't. Except when life hits me so hard that I can't get back up. Then I struggle not only with the actual condition itself but also with the sense that I've failed God, failed myself, and failed my family and friends. It's like being left alone in the middle of a wasteland with no help or even the *prospect* of help.

Church, we're looking at mental illness with distorted focus—spiritual astigmatism, if you will. We reserve our compassion and prayers for those who have "acceptable" ailments, as if an illness involving the mind must be one's own fault or is just too frightening to face. Even the term *mental illness* conjures up images of someone constrained in a straitjacket or receiving shock treatments.

The brain is a physical part of the body, just like the heart, lungs, muscles, or bones. It's subject to defects, damage, and alterations. Because it controls the functioning of the entire body, whole portions of our lives can be affected when it's ill or wounded.

Because mental illness is increasingly prevalent in our society, not only must we educate ourselves, but we must *also* create safe places where those who are suffering can find the spiritual and emotional support that's needed to fully recover or manage the condition. We must not allow our brothers and sisters in Christ to suffer silently and alone while the church looks over the top of her glasses with a disapproving stare.

Father, forgive me for judging what I don't fully understand. Help me to support my brothers and sisters who are suffering from mental illness. Lord, teach me to come alongside them through my prayers, my presence, and my practical support. And if my own spirit becomes crushed someday, please bring me those who have walked this path before me so that I don't face it alone.

Time to Steep

- Has there ever been a time in my life when I've walked through a season of depression? If not, do I know someone who has?
- What words and actions from others have strengthened and encouraged me during that time? How can I support someone who is suffering from depression?

For Further Steeping

Proverbs 18:14; Isaiah 53:3; Matthew 26:36–38; 2 Corinthians 1:3–5 and 8–9; 1 Corinthians 12:12–26; Psalm 9:9; Psalm 34:18; Psalm 42; Psalm 40:1–2

The Loneliest Hour

I was a stranger and you invited me in.

—Matthew 25:35c

We're all familiar with the routine. At some point in the worship service, the pastor instructs us to "greet the visitors." The congregation becomes a beehive of activity for somewhere between two and five minutes as people shake hands, exchange names, ask where you're from and if you're new, and then sit down and promptly forget most of what just took place. And a newcomer is supposed to feel welcome.

What does it *really* mean to welcome someone? As a person who has moved away from a church, from dear friends, and all that is familiar, I offer my thoughts.

Invite me into your home. I met one of my dearest friends and longest enduring friendships because a woman who greeted me as a visitor invited my family home to lunch after church that day. She doesn't even remember doing that, but I do. It made a huge impact on me. It was a spontaneous gesture of someone with a generous heart, who was willing to invite a stranger in and take a chance that something good might come of it.

Invite me into your life. When I was a newcomer to our church in Alaska, our pastor admonished the congregation to "undo some of our Legos" and make room for new people in our life. I was so grateful for his words because I felt like the invisible woman each Sunday as people walked past me to find their friends and interact with them. I wondered if anyone would ever have time for me or want to get to know me.

Invite me into your heart. We all carry joys and burdens both for ourselves and others, and sometimes we set a limit in our hearts without even realizing it. We limit our capacity to care. Inviting others into your heart means taking an interest in their lives, caring enough to break through the veneer of "How are you?" to find out what is *really* impacting them. It also means being transparent and vulnerable enough to share your struggles with *them*.

Does all this happen in those two to five minutes at church? No. It can't possibly. But if we're serious about making people feel welcome in our houses of worship, we need to shift the responsibility off of *them* trying to find a place to fit in and onto *us* making room for them—in our homes, in our lives, and in our hearts.

Father, help me reach outside my comfort zone to those who need welcome, friendship, and inclusion. Let me purposely create space in both my schedule and my heart to make room for the newcomer, the lonely, and the marginalized.

Time to Steep

- What can I do differently in my church to truly welcome the stranger?
- What do I need to let go of to make room in my life for new relationships?

For Further Steeping

Matthew 25:35–40; Galatians 6:2; Romans 12:13; 1 Peter 4:9; Hebrews 13:2

> "He asked her, 'Woman, why are you crying? Who is it you are looking for?' Thinking he was the gardener, she said, 'Sir, if you have carried him away, tell me where you have put him, and I will get him.' Jesus said to her, 'Mary.'"
>
> —John 20:15–16

I Meet Him in My Grief

Five Days a Grandma

Five days a grandma.
Five days marked with joy,
Looking toward the future of
A little girl or boy.

Will her hair be curly?
Will his eyes be blue?
Will her cheeks break into dimples
When I tell her "I love you"?

Only Jesus knows now.
He holds him in his arms.
Until we get to heaven,
Only angels see his charms.

She knows no pain or sickness.
Her life's not marred by sin.
Her Maker is her Father
Till the saints are gathered in.

So farewell, little grandchild,
But only for a time,
And when Grammy gets to heaven,
Then we'll read some nurs'ry rhymes.

Father, it hurts to know I will not hold this baby on this side of eternity. There is an ache in my soul that will not be soothed. The well-meaning platitudes of "You're young" or "You can have more" don't fill an empty heart and womb. I can only offer the comfort of my prayers, my understanding, and my own silent tears. Jesus, I know you understand; you're well *"acquainted with grief"* (Isaiah 53:3 NKJV). Lord, *heal our broken hearts* and bring an end to the pain.

Time to Steep

- Have I, or someone I've known, suffered the loss of a child or grandchild either before or after birth?
- How does the promise of eternal life ease my grief and give me hope?

For Further Steeping

Jeremiah 1:5; Psalm 139:13–16; Matthew 18:10; Isaiah 53:3 NKJV; Isaiah 61:1; Psalm 147:3; Revelation 21:4

Song for September

Verse 1:
Little bird with broken wings,
Will you find a place called home
Where loving arms enfold you
And you'll never be alone?
Will you find your heartsong
In the brightness of the day,
Or will it come in stillness
As the evening fades away?

Chorus:
Well, you think you'll never fly again,
But the Lord will carry you,
And though you try to understand,
All he asks is that you trust him with your pain.

Verse 2:
Little bird with broken wings,
Will you find a place called home
Where loving arms enfold you
And your destiny is known?
Will you find a windsong
Sent to take you far away?
Will you soar on heaven's voice
As he leads you day by day?

Chorus:
Well, you think you'll never fly again,
But the Lord will carry you,
And though you try to understand,
All he asks is that you trust him with your pain.

Bridge:
We only want to love you
Back to wholeness in our hands,
But your pain is so much with you
That you strike and strike again.

The Father calls you, and he's asking
You to trust,
To make a choice, each moment, that he's
Faithful and he's just.

Verse 3:
Little bird with mended wings,
Do you know he is your home?
His loving arms enfold you,
And he claims you as his own.
I hope you finally understand
You can trust him with your pain.
As he carries you,
You will surely fly again.
And as he carries you,
You will surely fly again.

Father, once again, I lift this wounded soul to your throne. I've watched more years pass with no answered prayers in sight. I know you're moving, though, because you've promised that "*[you cause] all things to work together for good to those who love [you], to those who are called according to [your] purpose*" (Romans 8:28 NASB). My heart longs to see her free, soaring as the one you created her to be.

Time to Steep

- Is there someone in my life who needs to be healed from heartache or restored to the Lord?
- Which scriptures can I meditate on to help me maintain endurance as I pray?

For Further Steeping

Deuteronomy 32:10–11; Psalm 28:9; Isaiah 40:11; Isaiah 46:3–4; Isaiah 63:9; Romans 8:28 NASB; Luke 18:1–8; Luke 11:5–13; Galatians 5:1a; Ephesians 6:18; 1 Thessalonians 5:17–18; 1 John 5:14–15

When Love Dies

Each heart knows its own bitterness.

—Proverbs 14:10

Betrayed
Destroyed
Death
Grief

Love, the GIFT, Rejected

Confused
Angry
Questions
Forgiveness
E
M
M
A
N
U
E
L

Father, you see all, and you know all. You know what it feels like to experience rejection and a loss of love. You know what it feels like when people you love so dearly turn away from you. Lord, I'm hurting intensely because I really invested myself and put my heart into building a relationship with this person. Father, I ask for your strength to forgive, and I ask you to heal my broken heart.

Time to Steep

- What is the most hurtful loss of love or friendship I've experienced?
- How can I draw comfort from the fact that God himself was rejected when he offered the gift of his own Son?

For Further Steeping

Proverbs 14:10; Psalm 41:9; Psalm 55:12–14; Isaiah 53:3–5; Psalm 34:18; Psalm 147:3

You Don't Owe Me

I release you from your debt.
You owe me nothing—
not an apology or an explanation,
neither gratitude nor love.

I've canceled your bill;
it's paid in full.
For the debt is so small
compared to mine.

As I was forgiven,
so I forgive you.
The prison door is open,
and we both walk free.

Father, I need your help to forgive. I know you've forgiven me more than I'll ever know—in fact, you forgive me daily. Give me the courage to act in faith and forgive the people who have wounded me, knowing and trusting that you will bring about justice coupled with mercy in every situation.

Time to Steep

- Is there someone in my life I'm struggling to forgive or even *refusing* to forgive?
- Is forgiveness the same as trust? How do I forgive a person from the heart but keep appropriate boundaries when necessary?

For Further Steeping

Matthew 6:12–15; Matthew 18:21–35; Mark 11:25; Ephesians 4:32; Colossians 2:14; Colossians 3:13; Psalm 89:14

Here Lies a Faithful Man

Philip Gene Roe

January 19, 1952 – June 6, 2006

At 6:30 in the morning, I woke up, donned my robe and slippers, and walked upstairs to the office. As was my habit, I checked my email first thing. I opened one from my dear friend, Linda, who had also sent me a chatty email the day before, which I needed to answer. Then I saw these words: "At 3:24 yesterday afternoon, Philip went to be with the Lord."

A shock ran through my body. My mind couldn't take it in. I read it a second time, and a wave of anguish crashed into my heart. I ran downstairs to tell my husband, barely able to speak through my sobs. My legs buckled.

It couldn't be, yet it was. A good and kind man, a man who loved God, a faithful husband and father of six children, was suddenly taken from this earth.

My thoughts raced to my friend and how I could comfort her, how soon I could get there, and what I could possibly say to explain the unexplainable. As I prayed for her and the children, the Lord quietly gave me this scripture: "The righteous perish, and no one takes it to heart; the devout are taken away, and no one understands that the righteous are taken away to be spared from evil. Those who walk uprightly enter into peace; they find rest as they lie in death" (Isaiah 57:1–2).

After attending the memorial, the funeral, and the burial over the weekend, I returned home with my husband. Then fear overwhelmed me. If a good man doing his job, faithfully going about his business, could not depend on the protection of the Lord, *then I was vulnerable too.* I suddenly felt like a little girl lost in a big department store.

All my Christian life, I had been taught that the Lord's protection was a *promise,* and even though I had seen evidence in the Bible, in my life, and in the lives of other Christians that we do suffer and sometimes even die prematurely, I was unprepared for this "in-your-face" failure of my flawed theology. Having lost one of my sisters to cancer only six months before Phil's death, the cumulative effect of this new grief threatened to drown me.

Over the course of the next three months, the Lord helped me to overcome my fear of the unexpected. He met me on the wrestling mat as I struggled with long-cherished beliefs and allowed him to heal my heart and form a new understanding of what it means for him to be my *Emmanuel*—God with us. He gave me peace in the midst of an uncertain world, and he taught me to cherish my moments and my days, not knowing how many I'll be given. He used the life of my brother in Christ to teach me to serve and work diligently until my time on earth is completed.

Phil, may you rest in peace, receiving the highest praise possible: "Well done, good and faithful servant!" (Matthew 25:21).

Father, I cannot begin to understand why some of your most faithful ones die prematurely. It is beyond me. It causes me to question your goodness and your ways, and I don't want to do that. Lord, help me accept the peace that comes from knowing you are Emmanuel—God who is with me, no matter what happens. Therein lies my security and trust.

Time to Steep

- How does someone's sudden, unexpected death threaten my own sense of security?
- Do my expectations about suffering or death agree with what I read in the Bible?

For Further Steeping

Psalm 116:15–16; Isaiah 57:1–2; Matthew 1:23; Psalm 139:16; Psalm 90:12; Matthew 25:21

While You Are Steeping

On the Passing of a New Friend

One month ago today, my friend, Lisa,[9] passed from this life into the next. Today, I remember and honor her.

Years ago, I watched a movie that included a scene where a garden club had gathered to view the opening of a rare flower that bloomed for only moments before withering. I was reminded of that today as I thought back on this last year of my friend's life.

For what seemed like minutes, she became part of my life. I saw the beauty of her spirit as she opened up to me, to my family, and to her Creator. In all too short a time, she was gone, and only the memory of the bloom remains.

Yesterday, a longtime friend gave me a sympathy card, apologizing for its lateness, yet acknowledging that maybe it was "right on time." She had included a copy of the page from her desk calendar from the day Lisa had died. The page quoted this passage from the Psalms:

> Yes, my soul, find rest in God; my hope comes from him. Truly he is my rock and my salvation; he is my fortress, I will not be shaken. My salvation and my honor depend on God; he is my mighty rock, my refuge. Trust in him at all times, you people; pour out your hearts to him, for God is our refuge.
>
> —Psalm 62:5–8

And so I pour out my heart to him, as he has invited me to do.

In Isaiah 53:3, the Bible describes the coming Messiah, whom we Christians have seen fulfilled in Jesus, as "a man of suffering, and familiar with pain." How thankful I am that God chose to come to

---

[9] The name has been changed to protect the privacy of the family.

earth in the form of a human and experience this life through my eyes. For how could I serve a God who knew nothing of my pain, my grief, my joys, or my challenges? How could I serve a God who chose to keep himself above the suffering of his creation?

Lisa is with the Lord now, beholding the beauty of his face and delighting herself in his goodness.

Today, dear friend, I honor you and I remember you. You were a joy to behold, if only for a moment.

Father, it's hard for me to understand why I have lost this friend to death. I was only beginning to know her. Yet for the time she was with me she touched and enriched my life, and she took me deeper into compassion and understanding. Thank you for the gift you gave me of this rare bloom, even though my season with her was brief.

Time to Steep

- How can I receive the gifts that the Lord wants to give me through someone who may not become a "forever friend"?
- In what situations do I need to depend on God as my rock, my fortress, my refuge?

For Further Steeping

Psalm 62:5–8; Isaiah 26:4; Psalm 61:2–4; Psalm 59:17; Psalm 46:1; Isaiah 53:3–5

At Year's End

I've just finished transferring birthdays, anniversaries, reminder notes, etc., to my new calendar. I've thrown away my old calendar with a mixture of relief and sadness.

As I mentally walked through the past 365 days again, I was reminded of more than appointments and annual celebrations. I was reminded of what a turbulent year it has been for all of us. It has been a year of sad endings and happy beginnings, losses and gains, crying and laughing. It has certainly been an "Ecclesiastes 3" year. Many of us have experienced devastation, whether in the loss of loved ones, the loss of health, or the loss of material things.

Recently, I've pondered a question that's been troubling me: How do you trust in an uncertain God—a God who doesn't always come through for you in the way you had hoped?

The God who *answers before I even call* supplied some insight that both expressed my heart *and* quieted it (Isaiah 65:24).

"Most often, I would rather not learn the hard lessons the hard way. I would rather not have to worship in the wilderness, where God continuously calls me to find and be found in Him. I would rather God simply meet my expectations, fix my problems, heal my hurts, and be on His way. I want a God who is faithful to me in ways I understand and expect, who expresses faithfulness in the ways I choose."[10]

"In Job's world, God was a question-answering god who faithfully provided wisdom. Yet when the God of Job finally appears, He only *asks* more questions. How disappointing for Job's friends. The God of Job clearly has more in mind than meting out justice.

---

[10] Michael Card, "God's Disturbing Faithfulness," *Discipleship Journal*, January–February 2005. Used with permission.

His faithfulness is expressed in a way that no one could have ever imagined: *He showed up!*

"Nothing could have been more disturbing for the lot of them." [11]

"God incarnate enfleshed and gave form to faithfulness. Faithfulness was Jesus fully present.

> "Present in their redemption and ours.
> "Present in their suffering and ours.
> "Present in their loneliness and ours.
> "Acquainted with their griefs and ours.

"This was a faithfulness no one expected—so deeply personal, so fully satisfying. Jesus didn't always faithfully give people answers or healing or judgments, but He did give them Himself." [12]

Father, forgive me for not realizing that your presence is the greatest gift you could ever give me. Forgive me for treating you like a genie in a bottle instead of the one who indwells me through your Holy Spirit. Lord, may I come to understand your faithfulness better in this new year, on *your* terms, not mine.

---

[11] Ibid.
[12] Ibid.

Time to Steep

- In what circumstances would I rather have someone just be with me than try to "fix things"?
- Why would I prefer to have God's power and provision, rather than his presence? What is the Lord revealing about *himself* in my current circumstances?

For Further Steeping

Ecclesiastes 3:1–8; Isaiah 65:24; Job 38–41; Matthew 1:22–23; John 11:1–44; Luke 24:13–35

While You Are Steeping

> "He called out to them, 'Friends, haven't you any fish?' 'No,' they answered. He said, 'Throw your net on the right side of the boat and you will find some.' When they did, they were unable to haul the net in because of the large number of fish. Then the disciple whom Jesus loved said to Peter, 'It is the Lord!'"
>
> —John 21:5–7a

I Meet Him in My Restlessness

I Wait

Lord of Abraham and Sarah,
Help me wait expectantly.
Let me not create an Ishmael
As impatience shadows me.

You have promised and confirmed
That you'll answer in your time.
May I place full confidence in you
And bind your hand to mine.

In this calm anticipation,
May your peace my cares constrain
Till I see the substance of my hope
And faith's refined again.

Father, it's so hard not to run ahead of you. Yet I think back on all the times I've taken matters into my own hands and how badly I've messed things up. I know that you are at work in me and the circumstances of my life, even as I wait. Please help me to rest in you.

Time to Steep

- In what ways am I still trying to "help" the Lord with a situation I've already surrendered to him in prayer?
- What good fruit have I seen produced in my life when I've waited patiently for the Lord instead of running ahead of him?

For Further Steeping

Genesis 16; Proverbs 3:5–6; Isaiah 40:31; Psalm 27:13–14; Lamentations 3:25–26; John 14:27; 1 Peter 5:6–7; 1 Peter 1:6–7; James 1:2–4; Galatians 6:9; Hebrews 11:1; Romans 8:25

Abba's Daughters

Faces hang in shame and fear,
Abba's daughters far and near;
Veiled in secrecy and lies,
Hiding pain from watchful eyes.

Who will set the young girls free,
Their babies resting on their knee?
Childhood barely graced their days
Till evil forced its wicked ways.

Abba hears their silent cries;
Heaven's witness testifies.
Rising from his throne, he calls,
"Who will scale the barrier walls?"

Mothers, sisters to their side!
Justice sprinting at full stride—
Passion pouring from your hearts;
Knowledge forming brand-new starts.

Who will set the young girls free?
His daughters wait for you and me.[13]

---

[13] This poem was written as a tribute to the girls kidnapped from Chibok. "Chibok schoolgirls kidnapping," Wikipedia, February 25, 2020, accessed March 5, 2020, https://en.wikipedia.org/wiki/Chibok_schoolgirls_kidnapping.

Father, when I read about the treatment of girls and women who have been abused, exploited, and trafficked, I want to run to their aid. Help me, Lord, not to turn a blind eye to their plight. Father, put a burden in my heart to intercede for them by the power of your Spirit. Show me the organizations and resources I can utilize so that I become your agent of restoration in their lives.

Time to Steep

- As I trust God more with my own life, how can I put "feet" to my faith by extending myself to help others?
- What steps can I take to secure God's justice or aid for a woman who has been abused or trafficked?

For Further Steeping

Psalm 146:5–9; Psalm 72:12–14; Isaiah 61:1; Isaiah 1:17; Proverbs 21:3; Proverbs 24:11; Proverbs 31:8–9; Psalm 82:3; 1 John 3:17–18; James 2:14–17; Psalm 106:3; Isaiah 58:6–11

On Earth As It Is in Heaven

Have you ever read the gospels and thought to yourself something like the following? "I *like* Jesus. He's so kind, so loving, so merciful. But *Father God* ... I don't know about him. I mean, I know Jesus said, 'Anyone who has seen me has seen the Father' [John 14:9], but when I read the Old Testament, I see a harsh, scary, oftentimes brutal God bent more on judgment than mercy. I just don't seem to relate well to the Father."

I know *I* have thought these same things before. And even as I've matured over the years, I still find myself recoiling when I read in the Old Testament about armies wiping out whole cities, the innocent along with the evil, about babies being dashed to the ground or pregnant women ripped open. It sounds as barbaric as anything I've read in the news.

I've never been able to explain away injustice with the theological platitudes that seem to comfort others: "His ways are higher than our ways" (Isaiah 55:9, paraphrased); "God works all things for good" (Romans 8:28, paraphrased); "God is sovereign" (e.g., Daniel 4:25c).

It's all true, but it doesn't necessarily comfort those of us who struggle with an oversized sense of justice or wrestle with the complexities and wickedness of this world.

As one who is often called to pray extensively for others, I've struggled at times with feeling like the persistent widow pleading before an "unjust judge" (Luke 18:2–8), knowing in my *head* that this is not the truth God was trying to convey to us through the parable, but feeling nevertheless that this was the kind of God I was presenting my case before.

In a lesson on prayer I've recently finished, Pastor Francis Frangipane explains a concept of intercession that I'd never heard before.

Frangipane writes honestly about the struggle shared by Christians and non-Christians alike in seeing *people* as more merciful and loving than God. When we pray, we often envision ourselves as being in a position of either talking God *into* something he seems reluctant to do or talking him *out* of something he seems set on doing.

Using the example of Jesus praying on earth to his Father in heaven, Frangipane explains that this is actually a picture of "God talking to God."[14] This reveals the ability of the Trinity to "remain one in nature yet separate in manifestation."[15]

Frangipane uses the example of Moses as intercessor, pleading for the nation of Israel each time God threatened to wipe them out. He states:

> For the spirit of intercession that emerged through Moses was not really Moses' spirit, but Christ's Spirit praying through him on man's behalf. This is significant: man, inspired by Christ, is the primary means through which God brings forth mercy to other men. What we are actually seeing operate through human instrumentality is God in His mercy interceding before God in His justice. At the highest level, intercessory prayer is God talking to God through man.[16]

This truth is liberating for me! When I'm moved to anger by an injustice I see or compelled to tears because of a human suffering, it's not my "good" human spirit crying out. It's the heart of God, through the Spirit of Christ in me, urging me to become God's agent of mercy in the situation through my intercession or my intervention.

---

[14] Francis Frangipane, *The Power of One Christlike Life* (Cedar Rapids, IA: Arrow Publications, 2011). Used with permission.
[15] Ibid.
[16] Ibid.

With this new understanding, I realize I'm not pitted against God in my prayers, trying to get him to change his mind. No, I'm appealing to a part of *God himself* as I pray. I speak from his mercy side, appealing to his justice side.

I, like many of you, have gravitated toward the Jesus of the gospels because it is *through* Jesus that we see *the merciful side of God*. But like an eternal canvas, his justice provides the background upon which his love is painted. Frangipane states:

> Without a doubt, God must reveal His righteous judgment concerning sin; otherwise, mercy has no meaning or value. God is revealed in the Godhead as Father, Son, and Holy Spirit. The Father is God manifesting Himself in authority and justice; Christ is God revealed in redemptive mercy; the Holy Spirit is God in manifest power, bringing forth in creative or destructive power the expressed will of the Godhead. The ultimate revelation of God is seen in the unveiling of perfect love; God's wrath is the backdrop.[17]

I have also struggled with the same question the world asks: "If God is such a loving God, why doesn't he *do* something?"

Frangipane addresses this burning question also. Just as we are called to be the expression of God's mercy through our urgent prayers for people and situations, we are also called to be the agents of God's provision for a wounded, suffering world. In so many ways, the unchurched have grasped this concept far better than God's people, for they instinctively respond to the injustices of this world, knowing that *unless someone acts,* nothing is likely to change.

Using Moses again as an example, Frangipane quotes the

---

[17] Ibid.

scripture in Exodus where God said to Moses regarding Israel, "I have seen the oppression ... I will send you ..." (3:9–10, NASB).

God works through people—what an obvious but misunderstood concept! As the church, we have longed to see the miraculous, sovereign intervention of God in the crises and miseries of this world. And so we should. Our prayers should be fervent as we lift up the needs of those around us. But along with that truth, we should also recognize that the passion of our hearts to make a situation right may also be a signal that we are to be the ones God *uses* to make it right.

This new understanding of prayer is going to be something I ponder over and over for a long time. I feel such a sense of excitement as I realize that "my" sense of justice is actually the heart-cry of God, longing to see a world gone mad transformed back into the Eden he created.

What this will mean for me in terms of the actions I pursue, I have yet to foresee. But my heart is compelled to echo Isaiah when he said, "Here am I. Send me!" (Isaiah 6:8c).

Father, thank you for revealing your heart to me and for helping me understand how the Trinity works in perfect unity. Thank you for showing me that justice and mercy are both facets of your divine character and that one gives meaning to the other. As your Spirit moves upon me to pray or to act, remind me that I'm your hands, feet, and mouthpiece on this earth. Help me to recognize when you are calling me to participate in your divine directives. I pray that you would develop in me a deep trust in you and your character as I see you at work and partner with you in the world.

Time to Steep

- Do I struggle with relating to Father God? If so, do I truly see Jesus as one with the Father or separate from him?
- How would it change my perspective to realize that the Holy Spirit moving through me as I pray is "God talking to God"?

For Further Steeping

John 10:30; John 14:9–11; Hebrews 1:3; Isaiah 55:9; Romans 8:28; Daniel 4:25c; Luke 18:2–8; Exodus 34:5–7; Psalm 89:14; Exodus 3:9–10; Isaiah 6:8c; Matthew 6:10; Romans 8:26–27

My Grown-Up Christmas

It's Christmas Eve, and there's a restless stirring in my heart. Something is missing, and I find myself grasping at the scriptures in search of it. Several times this Christmas season and in seasons past, I've heard people say, "Christmas is for the children," or "Christmas is about the children." Even in church. Well, if Christmas is for the children, then I'm certainly left out as a middle-aged empty nester. My children are grown and gone, and only one child will be home to visit this year. There are no grandchildren gracing my home yet and none on the horizon.

If Christmas is for the children, then perhaps our Christian traditions and celebrations are only a little less illusory than Santa and his reindeer. Perhaps we try to hold onto the magic and wonder we felt as children, hoping to rekindle those feelings through the memories we seek to recreate year after year. But if I can't have a grown-up Christmas, then why am I celebrating at all? If Christmas is only about "Away in a Manger" and not "O Come, O Come, Emmanuel," then perhaps I've missed the message entirely.

As I think about the gift of God that our heavenly Father sent to us so long ago, I realize that Christmas is about someone who had both the power and the resources to provide for a world without either, sending an emissary to make those resources available to us. Through Jesus, we've received what the Bible calls an "indescribable gift" (2 Corinthians 9:15). We've been given the gift of faith to believe in the one sent, so that we could receive the gift of eternal life; and we've been given the gift of the Holy Spirit so that we could have the power to live that life, which begins here on earth.

The Bible says that "Every good and perfect gift is from above, coming down from the Father of the heavenly lights" (James 1:17). As I think about the amazing gift that God sent to us, I realize that I have an opportunity at Christmas to do more than bless my friends and family with trinkets lovingly picked out for them. Certainly that's one expression of the love of God poured out. But beyond that, I realize that there's no better time of the year to magnify the message of God's heart to a broken and hurting world.

As I look at my life and my resources, I realize that I have much to offer others. I'm not talking about giving a token "guilt offering" so I can enjoy the bounty of Christmas. I'm talking about using my power and resources to impact a desperately needy world.

To those who are not in relationship with Christ, the message of Christmas is only a fleeting, feel-good story if it's not backed up by action. As Americans, we have wealth, knowledge, and influence only dreamed of in other parts of the earth. As Christians, we have the compassion of God flowing through us to direct those gifts to those who need it most. It's not governments that will solve the problems of this world; it's those of us who are under the government of Jesus Christ—citizens of heaven, sent as much to a helpless world as Jesus was.

This Christmas and beyond, may we seek out tangible and long-term ways to reach out to a suffering world with the message of hope and help that God initiated through sending his Son, Jesus Christ.

Father God, this is the time of year when millions become more aware of you and your Son, Jesus Christ. There's a pull, a hunger for peace, both within ourselves and among nations. We experience the gladness of goodwill toward others and the joy of generosity. Yet many of us find ourselves caught up in the trappings of culture and tradition, and the true message of your gift becomes obscured. Lord, *you gave that which is most dear to yourself because you loved us so much,* and it changed the course of mankind's history. Father, show me the ways—large and small—that I can demonstrate your love and change the course of someone's life.

Time to Steep

- How can I shift the focus in my giving from lavishing those who already have much to supplying those who have need?
- What time, talents, or treasures can I use to demonstrate God's love and help heal this broken world?

For Further Steeping

2 Corinthians 9:15; James 1:17; John 3:16; 1 John 4:9–10; Romans 5:8; Isaiah 9:6; Matthew 1:23; Philippians 3:20; John 17:18; John 20:21

I Cannot Fail

I watched a war movie with my husband last night about D-Day (the Normandy invasion), which focused on General Dwight D. Eisenhower.

Eisenhower, as you may remember, was named the Supreme Allied Commander in World War II. In an exchange between the Eisenhower and Churchill characters, Churchill tells Eisenhower, "All the same, between we two, surely God himself must tremble at the task that lies before you, and it is God's work you do, Ike. For you hold all our lives in your hands." Eisenhower replies, "If I do God's work, then he will be at my side, and I cannot fail."[18]

I marvel at the world they lived in versus the world we live in now, when even men and women who didn't necessarily profess faith in Jesus Christ had a pervasive sense of God's involvement in and through their lives. People understood the sovereign work of God in this world, and they were ready to fulfill their part in his plans.

This morning, I was reminded of what the book of Ephesians tells us: "For we are God's handiwork, created in Christ Jesus to do good works, which God prepared in advance for us to do" (2:10).

As I enter this new year, I'm asking God to lead me into those good works—and *only* those good works—*which he has prepared in advance for me to do.* For if I am doing God's work in the power of his Spirit, I cannot fail.

Father, I thank you that you are God in heaven and that you *rule and reign in the affairs of mankind* (Daniel 4:17). I thank you that even when the world looks like it's in complete chaos, your eternal plans

---

[18] *Ike: Countdown to D-Day,* directed by Robert Harmon, written by Lionel Chetwynd, aired May 31, 2004, on A&E.

are being accomplished. Thank you that I can trust your sovereignty in my life and the lives of those around me. Lead me into the work you've called me to do.

Time to Steep

- If I truly believed that God's eternal purposes will be accomplished and cannot be stopped by the actions of men and women, would I see events and circumstances in a different light?
- What good work do I sense the Holy Spirit leading me into, and what steps can I take to begin to walk in it?

For Further Steeping

Psalm 103:19; 2 Chronicles 20:6; Job 42:2; Proverbs 16:4 and 9; Proverbs 21:1; Daniel 4:17; Isaiah 14:24; Acts 5:38–39; Psalm 57:2 ESV; Ephesians 2:10

Epilogue

When God Is Silent

Dearest Friend,[19]

You've asked a very good question: "I don't understand how I can learn anything when God is silent. How is his silence valuable?"

There was a season in my life when it was particularly hard for me to live with what seemed like God's silence. Coming from a Christian background that places a strong emphasis on the outward expressions of the Spirit, I felt like there was no evidence of God in my life anymore.

I spent nearly a decade in this condition. Part of it arose from a very abusive spiritual situation that had taken place, from which I eventually healed. Part of it resulted from untreated clinical depression. But the part of it that was *God* was what produced good fruit in me over the long run.

I felt very alone because no one—not even those closest to me—understood what was happening with me or even what I was trying to describe to them. I went through the usual gamut of people trying to help me "look for sin" in my life, probe my psyche, "pray" me out of it, bind the enemy out of my life, and cram the Word into me; but nothing seemed to make a difference.

I would alternately run *from* God (because I was angry with him) or run *to* God out of desperation. I didn't understand what

---

[19] This was an actual letter written to a friend who was seeking answers.

was happening or why he was giving me the silent treatment. Still, I echoed Peter when he said, "Lord, to whom shall we go? You have the words of eternal life" (John 6:68).

It was only after I read about the silence of God in the lives of Christians in times past that I began to realize I was experiencing something that others knew about also. It just wasn't something modern Christians talked about often, or even understood.

That helped me calm down and realize that God was "*for [me]" and not against me* (Romans 8:31). I think that's a truth I had really struggled with the better part of my Christian life. I also began to learn about the sovereignty of God, something that had not been emphasized in my Christian church experience.

Along with these realizations, I began learning to trust God. I had to rely on him to lead me in ways that were neither familiar to me nor comfortable for me, and I didn't like it one bit! I had been taught to hear God primarily one way—by the "inward witness," by speaking to my heart, through that "gut feeling," or having peace about something I was considering. When God didn't accommodate me that way, it felt like he had taken my sight away. I truly felt like a blind woman groping for someone to lead me.

Because he stripped away his familiar way of speaking to me, I had to learn to receive from other people more. Until then, I had mainly relied on my own ability to hear from God, which I didn't realize had become a pride issue for me. Depending on others for spiritual guidance was humbling, and that wasn't a bad thing.

God also began to speak truth to me through Christian books and articles during that season. Though I was getting nothing out of church sermons, I would receive *a lot* from these publications. I decided this was okay; the truths I discovered as I read were as much God speaking to me as if I'd received them from the pulpit. This really expanded my ability to "hear."

I also began to pay more attention to circumstances that cropped up and how they related to my prayer life. I had learned from a Bible study to watch what happens after you pray, because that may often be the answer to your prayers. We tend not to think that way—we want something "spectacular" to happen to let us know it's God speaking. But I learned to recognize him more in the ordinary circumstances of my day.

At first, I found myself drawing a blank from the Bible when I read it. Though I had *studied* the Word a lot up until then, I had never been consistent in my Bible *reading*. I decided that I needed to read daily, whether I felt like I was getting anything out of it or not, but I didn't have much of a spiritual appetite. So I started with a little devotional book, and I graduated from there to a Bible reading plan. Developing this habit worked discipline into my life; it also developed a more well-rounded knowledge of the Bible than I had had before. I had always approached the Bible looking for "the new, the improved, the exciting" revelation! God taught me how to be faithful and consistent instead.

My prayer life was a tremendous struggle during that time. Sometimes I felt so angry at God I dared not even voice my thoughts. Yet I knew he knew them anyway, so I developed the art of being both genuine *and* respectful in my prayer times. For a long time, the only prayers I could pray were the ones in the Psalms. I would find a psalm that mirrored my feelings and would read it out loud to God. I'd tell him that was how I felt—kind of a "what he said" prayer. David's words jump-started my prayer life again so that I could eventually find my own words to pour my heart out to God.

I also learned to consistently incorporate worship into my personal time with the Lord. Sometimes I couldn't pray at all, but I could still sing, so that's how I would express my heart to God. In between songs, or after I was done, I would just sit in silence, knowing that God was there, even if he wasn't giving me any evidence of it.

Outwardly, I also learned to look for hallmarks of God all around me. I remember driving into town one time and seeing the sun reflecting off the mountains in an incredible way, and I said out loud, "Wow, God! You did an *awesome* job on that!" I began to do this a lot, noticing his hand everywhere.

After a long, long time—nearly a decade—the Lord graciously

restored my ability to *feel* his presence again. Perhaps I was fully healed, or perhaps his work was fully accomplished.

I developed much more compassion for people during this time and learned not to be judgmental when people were going through their own hard times. I realized that I seldom had the whole picture of why people do the things they do or respond in certain ways. I learned to pray more and judge less.

As trite as it sounds, I learned to "wait for the dawn." It really does always come. I learned endurance and perseverance through these hard times.

I believe that my relationship with the Lord is much richer and much deeper for having gone through that horrible decade. I hope I never have to go through that experience again—once in a lifetime ought to be enough—but I learned I can survive a long spiritual drought, and I learned to sink my roots down even deeper. I learned that even when the riverbeds run dry, there is a well of life that's always full that I can continue to draw from.

Every so often, God does lift the ability to feel his presence. Sometimes it's because there is something sinful in our lives and he needs to get our attention, but at times, it's because he's teaching us to just trust his love and trust that he is there and has not abandoned us, even when we can't sense him. My friend, you only learn from hardships if you *choose* to learn. If you choose not to learn, then you only end up bitter. Only you can decide the outcome of the particular suffering or discipline God has uniquely chosen in order to build into you the character of Christ. God *is for you and not against you,* but his ultimate goal for you is not just for you to be "happy." His ultimate goal for this lifetime is that you look like Jesus in the end. When I learned that lesson, my life seemed a lot less unfair and started to make more sense.

Much love,

Rebecca

References

Broughton, Chuck. "Fruit Without Frustration." *Discipleship Journal*, May–June 2005. Used with permission.

Card, Michael. "God's Disturbing Faithfulness." *Discipleship Journal*, January–February 2005. Used with permission.

Frangipane, Francis. *The Power of One Christlike Life*. Cedar Rapids, Iowa: Arrow Publications, 2011. Used with permission.

Harmon, Robert, dir. *Ike: Countdown to D-Day*. Written by Lionel Chetwynd. Aired May 31, 2004, on A&E.

Lemmel, Helen Howarth. *The Heavenly Vision (Turn Your Eyes Upon Jesus)*. 1918. Public domain.

Merriam Webster Online Dictionary. *Steep*. https://www.merriam-webster.com/help/citing-the-dictionary (accessed November 7, 2019).

Perrin, Cathy, and Wayne Perrin. *When I Look into Your Holiness*. ©1981. Integrity's Hosanna! Music. Used with permission.

The New American Webster Handy College Dictionary. 3. The Penguin Group, 1995. Copyright © Philip D. Morehead and Andrew T. Morehead, 1995. Published by The Penguin Group. First Published by Signet, an imprint of New American Library, a division of Penguin Putnam, Inc.

The NIV Study Bible New International Version. Copyright © 1985 by Zondervan. Used by permission of Zondervan. www.zondervan.com.

Wikipedia. 2020. *Chibok schoolgirls kidnapping.* February 25. Accessed March 5, 2020. https://en.wikipedia.org/wiki/Chibok_schoolgirls_kidnapping.